Fun at Six

by Samantha Taylor
illustrated by Hiro Kimura

Practice Decodable 9

McGraw Hill Education

Bothell, WA • Chicago, IL • Columbus, OH • New York, NY

MHEonline.com

Send all inquiries to:
McGraw-Hill Education
8787 Orion Place
Columbus, OH 43240

ISBN: 978-0-02-143434-3
MHID: 0-02-143434-4

Printed in the United States of America.

8 9 10 CTM 23

Jan did not run at six.

But Jan can spin!

Jan can spin just for fun.

Jan must spin up for a cup.

But Jan can spin fast.

Jan can spin up past Max.